D0674090

YOU KNOW YOU'RE A CHILD OF THE

'80s

WHEN...

MARK LEIGH
MIKE LEPINE

summersdale

YOU KNOW YOU'RE A CHILD OF THE '80s WHEN...

Copyright © Summersdale Publishers Ltd, 2004

Reprinted 2006

Text by Mark Leigh and Mike Lepine

Summersdale Publishers Ltd
46 West Street
Chichester
West Sussex
PO19 1RP
UK

www.summersdale.com

Printed and bound in Belgium

ISBN: 1-84024-550-6
ISBN: 978-1-84024-550-9

Mark Leigh

Born in 1966, Mark spent most of his formative years in the 1980s and admits to still possessing designer stubble, a pair of stone-washed jeans and two Nik Kershaw albums. Mark's biggest regret is not having a snog at the college disco with Daisy Duke, Nena or that girl from Roxette. He is currently building a time machine.

Mike Lepine

Mike spent the 1980s being baffled at all the criticism hurled at Maggie Thatcher, since it was patently obvious to him that everyone had loads of money and was having a good time. Living in Blairite Britain has only made him more determined to see Maggie back in power, no matter how ga-ga she is now.

A big thank-you for assistance / ideas / putting up with us while the book was being written, to the following: Philippa Hatton-Lepine; Debbie, Polly and Barney Leigh; Andrea Hatton; Martin Wheat; Liz Kershaw; Kerry Parker, and Fran Connop (a true child of the '80s).

You know you're a child of the '80s when...

You didn't think there was anything intrinsically mental about going out on a Saturday night wearing a head-to-toe tartan ensemble finished off with a purple sash.

The four biggest influences on your life were Mrs Thatcher and Stock, Aitken and Waterman.

You once really believed that boys found puffball skirts and pixie boots sexy.

You fantasised about a threesome with Pepsi and Shirley and a fivesome with The Bangles.

You learned all you
needed to know
about self-defence
from watching
The Karate Kid.

... and all you needed to know about sex from *Just Seventeen*.

You asked your careers teacher about opportunities as a Top Gun, a Ghostbuster or an American Gigolo.

You remember parties starting with a six-pack of Double Diamond and a bottle of Liebfraumilch and ending with the contents regurgitated all over your shoes.

Your party piece
is doing Rubik's
Cube in under 40
seconds. That or
reciting all the
words to 'Vienna'.

You were beaten
up just for having
a haircut like
that bloke
in A Flock of
Seagulls.

You found the woman dancing to the titles of *Tales of The Unexpected* erotic (and still do).

Your first experience of a 'celebrity chef' was Rustie Lee.

You wished you could own something by Sergio Tacchini, let alone spell it.

You understand what's meant by a seven-inch single and a C60 cassette.

Your dream car at the time was an XR3i cabriolet and your dream job was a Eurobond salesman. (Or the lead guitarist in Bon Jovi.)

You wished your dad was Jan Michael-Vincent from *Airwolf* and your mum was Maria Whittaker.

You remember dying to get back to school on a Monday morning so you could talk about *The Young Ones.*

Your collection of mint condition *Transformers* toys is worth far more now than your endowment mortgage.

'George Michael' makes you think of WHAM! rather than LA policemen.

You used to have Big Hair. Now you're glad to have any.

**Your role models
were Gordon Gekko,
Donald Trump
and Tucker from
Grange Hill.**

Video Nasties were big news – and something you can watch nowadays most nights of the week on Channel 5.

The contents of your entire childhood can be seen every Sunday, spread out across a trestle table in a car boot sale (there, or on the pages of e-Bay).

You used to pretend that your BMX bike was the Millennium Falcon (and your older sister was Chewbacca).

Your motto then was 'Girls Just Wanna Have Fun'.

You made a 'Charles and Di Royal Wedding' scrapbook at school.

You can name
all the individual
Thundercats.

You'd never heard of Global Warming or CFCs and what's more, couldn't give a toss as long as your hair was rock solid when you went clubbing.

Partying like it was 1999 once seemed an eternity away.

You don't remember a time when drinking coffee was a cool thing to do (and if you do remember, then you don't recall having 27 different types to choose from).

De rigueur footwear was velcro Reebok Hi-Tops worn with the laces undone (and jeans tucked in).

You wanted to marry Michael J Fox because, at the time, he was the same height as you.

You used to say, 'By the power of Greyskull, I am He-Man!' – and believe it might work.

You remember
foods that weren't
preceded by the
letters 'Mc'.

The Care Bears and the Smurfs were on your Christmas list (and not because you thought they were ironic).

Jennifer Beales in *Flashdance* **was the most erotic thing you'd ever seen until it was revealed recently that a man did most of the dancing on the screen.**

You would rather go barefoot or stomp around in cereal boxes than wear the trainers your mum bought from British Home Stores.

You thought (well, for two weeks, anyway) that Vanilla Ice was cool.

Being called a Yuppie was something to be proud of.

You thought that Toyah was a one-woman feminist revolution.

You remember
actually laughing
at Timmy Mallet,
Hale and Pace
and Ben Elton.

You owned more
pairs of bleached
denim jeans
than Kim Wilde.

You thought the
most knowledgeable
authorities on
pop music were
Bruno Brookes,
Jakki Brambles
and Peter Powell.

Your make-up bag contained an almost limitless supply of electric-blue eye shadow and neon lipstick.

Miss World was
essential viewing.

You took all your
fashion cues from
Don Johnson
or Madonna.

A computer screen that displayed more than 16 colours wasn't just unusual, it was science fiction.

You can trace your coming of age to the exact moment when the girls in Bucks Fizz whipped off their skirts.

You remember when there were movies that weren't based on old TV series.

You wished *you* were the girl in that A-ha video for 'Take On Me'.

You slapped your sister after arguing who was better looking in *CHiPs*: Ponch or Jon.

You used Tipp-Ex (and immediately wished you hadn't) to make that stripe on your face, just like Adam Ant.

You're depressed that when you fill in forms, you now have to tick the box marked '25–35' (or worse).

Your mum let you stay up late just so you could watch the x-rated version of the 'Thriller' video.

If you haven't already had it, you're starting to really dread your 30th birthday.

You remember when *American Gigolo* was raunchy... and *Porky's* was funny.

You didn't give a toss about who shot JR, but you remember wishing someone would murder Roland Rat.

Shop assistants now call you Sir or Madam (and you don't like it).

You got your first grope at the school disco, snogging to Spandau Ballet's 'True'.

You remember
buying Now That's
What I Call Music 1.

You can sing the chorus to 'Physical' by Olivia Newton-John.

You owned a T-shirt that featured Toto's tour dates on the back... or a large smiley face on the front.

You had a mullet to rival those sported by DJ Pat Sharp and singers Paul King and Limahl.

Your perfume of choice was Poison or Giorgio Beverly Hills, and people knew you were coming twenty minutes away.

You remember all the names of Five Star. (OK. They were Stedman, Lorraine, Delroy, Deniece and Doris.)

You bitterly recall being made to feel a social pariah because you had a Betamax VCR.

You learned everything you needed to know from reading *The Face*.

You remember exactly where you were when you heard that Kajagoogoo had split up.

No matter what
people say, a part
of you still believes
that a thin leather
tie with a piano
keyboard printed
on it looks cool.

You wanted to marry Tiffany and Debbie Gibson.

You remember a time when you had to get up off the sofa and walk over to the TV to change channels.

Your idea of sophistication was chicken kiev accompanied by a glass of Piat d'Or.

You were off school for two weeks after dislocating your shoulder break-dancing.

At the office
Christmas party
you still prefer
body-popping to
a slow dance with
that busty girl
from Accounts.

You think that a Palm Pilot is a flash in the pan and that nothing will replace your trusty Filofax.

Your social life used to centre around *Trivial Pursuit* and *Pictionary*.

Your shoulders sported pads large enough to land a helicopter on.

You can reminisce
for hours about
Knotts Landing,
Falcon Crest
and *Hotel*.

Even today you wish your company Vauxhall Vectra could talk just like KITT from *Knight Rider*.

**Your first
introduction to
foreign cuisine was
a Vesta dehydrated
chop suey.**

You're now desperately trying to get *Footloose*, *St Elmo's Fire* and *War Games* on DVD.

You were sent to your room after watching *Fame* and dancing on the bonnet of your dad's Mini Metro.

Thanks to *Desperately Seeking Susan* you still have to fight the urge to dry your armpits with a hot air dryer.

You once scored top marks in the *Look In* 'How Well Do You Know Shakin' Stevens?' quiz.

You were savvy
enough to know that
Frankie Knuckles
was a Chicago
house DJ and
not an associate
of the Krays.

You believed the hype about Sigue Sigue Sputnik.

**Your first
personal stereo
was at least twice the
size of this book.**

You Know You're a Child
of the '60s When...

Mark Leigh &
Mike Lepine

£4.99

ISBN: 1-84024-515-8
ISBN: 978-1-84024-515-8

Would you know a Mod from a Rocker, Dr No from
Dr Who, or Simon from Garfunkel? If so, then kick
off your go-go boots, switch on the lava lamp and
reminisce about the age of peace and free love, when
England won the World Cup, men walked on the moon
and Daleks first menaced the planet.

You Know You're a Child
of the '70s When...

Mark Leigh &
Mike Lepine

£4.99

ISBN: 1-84024-516-6
ISBN: 978-1-84024-516-5

Did you ride a Chopper to school, buy your dad Old
Spice for Christmas or believe that Jim could really fix
it? If this sounds like you then hang up your disco ball,
rake out the old Atari 2600 and tuck into a curly-wurly
as you prepare to find out if you are a true child of the
70s in this flashback to the decade that style forgot.

www.summersdale.com